Songs of the Sons & Daughters of Buddha

SONGS OF THE SONS & DAUGHTERS OF BUDDHA

TRANSLATED BY

Andrew Schelling & Anne Waldman

ILLUSTRATED BY *Robert Schelling*

SHAMBHALA

Boston & London

1996

Shambhala Publications, Inc.
Horticultural Hall
300 Massachusetts Avenue
Boston, Massachusetts 02115

Some of these poems have appeared in *Bombay Gin, Colorado Quarterly,
Cottonwood, Napalm Health Spa, Shambhala Sun, Sulfur,* and *Tricycle: The Buddhist
Journal.* Others were published in book form by O Books and Rodent
Press. Gratitude to the editors of those publications. We would like to
thank a few others: Robert Schelling for his illustrations, The Naropa
Institute's librarian Ed Rutkowski for bibliographic assistance, and our
editor at Shambhala, Peter Turner.

9 8 7 6 5 4 3 2 1

First Edition
Printed in Canada
♾ This edition is printed on acid-free paper that meets
the American National Standards Institute z39.48 Standard.
Distributed in the United States by Random House, Inc.,
and in Canada by Random House of Canada Ltd

Library of Congress Cataloging-in-Publication Data
Tipiṭaka. Suttapiṭaka. Khuddakanikāya. Theragāthā. English. Selections.
Songs of the sons and daughters of Buddha / Andrew Schelling
and Anne Waldman. —1st ed.
p. cm.
Includes bibliographical references.
ISBN 1-57062-172-1 (alk. paper)
I. Schelling, Andrew. II. Waldman, Anne. III. Tipiṭaka. Suttapiṭaka.
Khuddakanikāya. Therigāthā. English. Selections. IV. Title.
BQ1442.E54S25   1996   95-30054
294.3'823—dc20   CIP

Honor to the Exalted One,
Arhat, Buddha Supreme!

As you would tune
your ear
to the sharp-tooth'd lion's roar
echoing deep
in the mountains—
listen
to the songs of these
disciplined ones
telling their names, their lives,
how they hungered for Dharma
how they struggled to
      freedom

Sharp, they lived
without staggering—
enough simply to see a vision
it glints here
      it glints there—
and so they touched the ageless unborn Way
so they lived
and so they set to song
the brave details
      of their search

                  —DHAMMAPALA

This planet's ancient forests have long provided shelter for poets and recluses. The very books in which our poems and writings take sanctuary come into being at the expense of countless trees. In honor of the Buddhas of old, we dedicate this book to the many individuals and organizations at work on the preservation and conservation of forests.

Contents

Songs of the Daughters of Buddha

Preface

WHAT YOU HOLD IN YOUR HANDS is a translation of selected poems from the early Buddhist scriptures entitled *Theragatha* and *Therigatha*. The two books are preserved in the Pali scriptures, the earliest written documents known to Buddhism. They did not, however, get put into written form, which is to say transcribed onto palm leaf, until a great Buddhist council took place in Sri Lanka during the reign of King Vattagamani (circa 89–77 BCE), centuries after the poems were first composed. Many are ascribed to direct disciples of Gautama Buddha, which means they had been in circulation for 350 years before finding their way into written form.

These *gatha* (songs or poems) thus formed part of a vast oral tradition, preserved in memory and passed from person to person for generations. Scholars believe the language spoken in the early Buddhist community was Magadhi, a vernacular of northern India. By the time the first written documents of Buddhism appeared, the spoken language had changed considerably and grammarians had formalized some of its conventions. Over the years, then, these poems must have shifted, developed, gathered new material, lost stanzas that seemed obsolete, even been corrected for grammatical imprecisions. Philosophers doubtless adjusted the contents to reflect an evolving sophistication of Buddhist thought. Dogmatists probably expunged much that did not meet their own peculiar needs for consistency. So, the surviving written texts may well stand at some great distance from the living, breathing, spirit of the songs originally sung by these early austere contemplatives.

Our effort as translators has been to restore the spark and excitement of the poetry that ripples beneath the canonical text. Composed out of intricate, often terribly difficult lives, the old poems reveal textured human existences. Where our versions depart from the Pali texts, they do so because we have tried to eliminate unnecessary repetitions within the poems (you might call them tag lines), as well as obtuse material no longer accessible without some sort of in-depth notation. We have also tried to sniff out some of the later formulaic stuffing put in by scholastics of the Buddhist world. The first person we know of to suggest that some kind of doctoring of the poems must have occurred was the estimable Victorian scholar Caroline Rhys Davids, in a curious little book that inquired what might be covered up by the dry, sententious, and repetitious formulas that so often conclude a wildly enchanting poetic performance. Along with her troubling and useful questions, Rhys Davids also produced the first complete, methodical translations of the *Theragatha* and *Therigatha* into English. We have consulted her rigorous but eccentric efforts with gratitude, consternation, awe, and often amusement. (For a complete list of books we have worked with, including editions of the original Pali, see the bibliography.)

In our attempt to sound out the living voices of these notable poets, and to free them from what in Zen is called "the stink of religion," our first task was to let the personality of each poem breathe. This project began ten years ago when Anne Waldman was a graduate student in the Buddhist Studies program at The Naropa Institute and Professor Judith Simmer-Brown directed her attention to the neglected women poets, the *theri*, of early Buddhism. Inspired by the *theri*'s poetic devotions, Andrew Schelling brought his familiarity with old India's poetic traditions to the task of translating the *thera*—the men.

While these poems still lived on the tongue, prior to their transcription onto palm leaf, a scholar-poet named Dhammapala arranged them in the order in which they have come down to us. Dhammapala drew on the stories and lore of his day and wrapped many of the poems in anecdotal commentaries to explain the occasions on which the poems were initially sung. Even in his day a great many of the poems must have seemed obscure without the little narratives full of folklore, hagiography, and historical color that set the stage for them. Where we felt it necessary, we have added whatever of Dhammapala's commentary seems worth retelling, especially when indispensable to an understanding of the poems. As Buddhists consider only the poems canonical and not the commentary, we have used Dhammapala only where his words seem vital to the poems themselves. If we have made a contribution to the tradition, it is to free these old ones—buried under centuries of piety and scholasticism, not always well served in translation—to breathe once again.

In the Pali texts the originals have no titles—a heading simply notes the singer's name. We have taken the liberty of occasionally devising titles that convey hints concerning the poets and their utterances. This is one way to differentiate the various poems. Modern readers are unfamiliar with the cast of characters, but remember, most of these poets once were well-known figures in Buddhist history and folklore. Some were close disciples of Buddha Shakyamuni, and all were members of the fledgling community of practitioners formed while the Buddha lived. Try not to think of them as monks and nuns, which is how modern scholars often speak of them. They lived as members of a wandering mendicant order. In their day Buddhism had no established centers, no monasteries, no temples. Having renounced secular lives, these poets lived on the road; they slept in fields, forests, city parks, and caves. They begged their food, performed austerities, and invented a song or two about their experiences.

A Note on Spelling

Except for proper names and the terms *bhikkhu* and *bhikkhuni*, which we have kept in the original Pali, most Buddhist terms appear here in their Sanskrit forms, which are more familiar to Western readers. We have included a glossary of all such terms.

Songs of the
Sons of Buddha

Mahakala Speaks

This lady who cremates the dead
black as a crow—
she takes an old corpse and breaks off a thighbone,
takes an old corpse and breaks off a forearm,
cracks an old skull and sets it out
like a bowl of milk
for me to look at

Witless brain don't you get it—
whatever you do just
ends up here
Get finished with karma, finished with rebirth—
no more bones of mine
on the slag heap

Gangatiriya Speaks

I made a hut
from three palm leaves by the Ganges,
took a crematory pot
for an eating bowl,
lifted my robe off a trash bin
Two rainy seasons passed and I
spoke only one word
Clouds came again
but this time the darkness
tore open

Jambuka

Born in this Buddha-age to a rag-picking family, driven by old karma, Jambuka took to feeding on excrement. He declared himself a "sky-clad" or naked ascetic, left home, and for decades ate nothing but beans—one by one from the point of a straw. When he had reached the age of fifty-five, his wanderings brought him close to the Buddha, who noticed, like a lamp glinting within a jar, enlightenment in that dark heart. The Buddha approached, spoke gently, and with the words "Come, Bhikkhu!" drew him onto the Path.

In his last hours, Jambuka composed this poem:

> I plastered myself
> with grime and road dust for
> fifty-five years,
> eating food once a month
> plucking each hair as it sprouted
> from my face
> or my scalp
> I practiced terrible yogas—
> stood for days on one leg
> slept on rock
> fed myself shit and scowled
> at whoever came near

Those actions like an irresistible
flood swept me to
ruin and grief
But I've made wisdom my own now
I took refuge in Buddha
I have accomplished
what was to be done

Matangaputta Speaks

Too cold, too hot,
too late in the evening—
with words like these
men quit early and miss their chance
Don't they get it—
cold and hot are wild grasses
I push through furze, gorse, whin, broom—
spear grass, ribbon grass
I sit in the bulrushes alone

Bhaddaji

Where is that king Panada—
built a pillar of gold ore
sixteen arrows across,
a thousand arrow-lengths tall
A thousand long arrows tall
and hung with a hundred gold ornaments
Covered with banners,
built it from gold,
and surrounded it with ten thousand
dancers . . .
Where is that king Panada now?

Kottitha

Dead to the world and its troubles
he recites mantras
        mind unruffled
shaking distractions away
like the wind god
scatters a few
        forest leaves

Mahanama

Reborn in this Buddha-age to a brahmin clan at Savatthi, Mahanama joined a company of monks after hearing the Enlightened One speak. Hungry for insight he scaled Hunter's Point to meditate, but a host of ugly thoughts and painful desires swarmed over him. "What good is life with a mind so wretched?" he cried, and climbed a steep crag in disgust. "I'll kill him!" he shouted, as though it were somebody else, and preparing to throw himself down muttered this verse:

> Agh! What a ghastly
> end you've brought yourself to,
> Mahanama,
> your grave a desolate
>   cliff at Hunter's Point
> smothered with *sal* trees
> and tangled with brush—

As he stood cursing over the cliff's edge, working up courage to cast himself off, an abrupt and unshakable insight tore through him. Thus Mahanama became an *arhat*.

Nandaka Meets His Wife

One day Nandaka was wandering in search of alms through the town of Savatthi, when he met his former wife face to face. She gave a little laugh, an amorous little laugh, remembering the nights he had shared her bed. Divining her thoughts, Nandaka lectured her on Dharma, emphasizing repugnance for the body and cautioning how Mara the tempter sets his snares.

> That wretched malodorous thing,
> that woman's body,
> its nine streams always leaking—
> piss, shit, blood and tears
> cum, saliva, snot
> thin milk and
> sweat—
>
> Yet you smirk
> over past conquests and imagine
> it might lure a son
> of Buddha?
> Sex in heaven couldn't sway this beggar,
> how much less what's
> done on earth?

Instruments of Mara these
legs and arms,
hips, breasts and sex—
Mara sets out
charms
to snare dark hearts and
       muddy minds

But there are men untouched by lust
or ignorance,
who've got
no appetite for leaky
sweating bodies
These ones have cut the cords, woman,
       these have gotten free

Belatthakani Observes

Abandoning his house,
mind just drifting,
rooting his snout through mud
like an impatient hog—
here comes the fool
flickering through yet another
     womb

Candana Speaks

Draped with gold fabric
a child on her hip
her troop of maids trailing behind her
I saw my baby's
mother
come through the charnel field
    toward me

O evil snare—
I saw cause and effect approach
I saw in her gait the root
of suffering—
but I've gone
the way the ancient buddhas went
    I'm out of reach

The Monk Gotama

I fared
through realms of samsara
born again and again
in foul hungry-ghost lands—
oh agony, I dropped
from animal wombs of every shape
one after another
Eagerly I took human form
eagerly the occasional rebirth
in heaven
Worlds of form
unformed worlds
worlds between consciousness
and oblivion, drifted . . .
I saw them all
saw how
empty this coming to birth after birth
the flicker of wombs
born of conditions, contingent
drifting, unstable
I saw how this feverish self
comes to existence
realized it all and can say—
this is what drives a man
      to quiescence

Sundara-Samudda Resists

At a festival Sundara-Samudda's mother saw young men and women sumptuously dressed. She thought of her son's ragged renunciant cloak and wept. A young prostitute comforted her and promised to entice Sundara back. The mother offered, should the girl succeed, to make her mistress of the family. Going forth in a fragrant robe, with jewels and golden slippers, the girl approached Sundara. She stepped from her slippers and cast him an inviting look. The boy shivered with desire. This is his poem:

> Got up in silk and flowers,
> jewels on her breasts,
> her feet stained crimson with powder and shod in
> little gold slippers
>
> A prostitute
> slipped from her shoes
> Standing in front of me
> with cupped hands she said
>
> "You are young to have gone forth
> young for Buddha's precepts
> Stay awhile and learn
> the rules and precepts I follow,
> I'll teach you to love

"Love is the sweetest precept,
do you doubt it?
I'll fetch fire and make an oath on the flame—
I'll teach you about love

"Ah and then, when we've gotten toothless, old,
decrepit, leaning on staffs,
too wobbly for sex
we can go forth together—
Think it over
either way it's a winning throw"

When I saw that prostitute cup her hands
heard her plead
smelled her robe and perfumes
it was a snare of death at my feet

A deeper hunger shook me,
I saw cause and effect come into focus,
my mind fought free—
On the spot I conquered three knowledges

O I did what Buddha taught me

Ratthapala Rebukes the Women and Instructs a King

With great difficulty Ratthapala obtained his parents' permission to join the order of *bhikkhus.* He studied diligently and conquered his passions, then returned to his hometown to beg alms. At his father's house rancid gruel was ladled into his bowl, but he fed upon it as though on ambrosia. The ladies of the house, decked out in splendor, came forward and taunted him: "What are the ladies of heaven like, O Lord, the ones who enjoy your devotion?" Ratthapala rebuked them for their conduct with a poem.

> Look at the painted marionette
> blistered with sores
> a diseased compounded thing of
> schemes and ideas—
> utterly unstable
>
> See its paint job,
> jewels, earrings, see how it's covered
> with bone and skin
> fancy clothes
> to make it fine

See its foot soles, reddened with lac
its ointment-smeared face
O it can delude a fool
but not a person who seeks the far shore—

Eight braids in its hair
collyrium ringing the pits of its eyes
it can delude a fool
but not a person who seeks the far shore—

Like a painted collyrium pot
gorgeously embossed
full of muck on the inside
it can delude a fool
but not a person who seeks the far shore—

Did you notice the hunter
setting his trap?
The deer chewed up its fodder but avoided
the snare—
let's go while the trapper laments

The hunter's trap is broken
the deer steps far off at
the margin—
let's go while the trapper laments

Ratthapala's father ordered servants to bolt the house's seven doors, seize the renunciant, strip off his saffron robe, and dress him in white. But Ratthapala flew through the sky to King Koravya's Antelope Park and landed on a stone slab. Hearing of his arrival, the king went into the park and asked Ratthapala, "Master, men renounce the world because some disaster hits—disease, bankruptcy, loss of a child. You've suffered nothing like that, so why have you abandoned the world?" Ratthapala replied, "The world is transient, it passes away, there is no refuge."

> I see rich men in the world
> deluded they hang
> onto money
> heap up wealth in their greed
> and crave only pleasure
>
> A king who's conquered every acre of land
> up to the sea
> gets restless and bitter
> he can't rest till he's taken
> the distant shore also
>
> Not just a king but
> any man
> arrives at death twisted with craving
> sheds his body
> but still hasn't tasted enough pleasure

Relatives mourn him
their hair matted with grief, they cry in bewilderment
"He wasn't immortal!"
and carry him out in a shroud
build a pyre
and immolate him

He is burnt
prodded with insulting long poles
he's wrapped in a sheet but his wealth stays behind
Friends, relatives, neighbors—
no one protects him

Heirs take his money and land
the dead creature
takes only his karma along
Wealth doesn't follow a dying man
children don't, wife, riches, not even a kingdom

You can't purchase longevity
can't beat off old age with gold
the wise have told us how
short life is
how subject to change

Everyone's touched—
rich or poor

wise man or fool, all are touched
the fool falls to his knees
but the wise man when touched
doesn't tremble

Think of it
a man comes to the womb
enters a world
we call it samsara
some other man follows the first
and enters a womb as well—

Foolish men
born again and again
and still they accumulate karma

Think of it
a thief caught at the door
gets beaten
for what he's done
At the door of life a man gets beaten
for what in a previous
life he's done

Animal pleasures, seductive and sweet
endlessly trouble the mind
I saw the peril, O King
and went forth

Fruit falls from a tree
men also fall, their bodies young or old
         broken husks—
O King, I saw the peril
so I went forth

My venturing forth bore fruit, O King
I eat without debt
I regard sex as a scorching flame
gold I see as a knife
I've seen how the moment you enter a womb
it all leads to pain
and how the hells are dreadful

Seeing it all
I felt terror once, I felt distress,
then a sudden calm took hold of me—
I put down my load
and followed Buddha's teaching

O King, I have attained the goal
for which I went into the homeless state—

I have annihilated the fetters

The Monk Kulla

I entered the burial ground
and saw
flung into a grave
a female body mangled by worms.
Look, Kulla—
an oozing corpse,
foul, dripping, exuding vapors
Only a fool delights in bodies

Grasping Buddha's teachings like a mirror
I studied the corpse
hollow within,
        hollow without

This body here, that body there
that one like this and this like that—
As above, so below,
as below, so above,
As by day, so by night,
as by night, so by day,
I stared in the mirror and saw
this body here
        that body there—

O Kulla! even the five great
musical notes
can't give such joy as a mind fixed on
    Buddha's teachings!

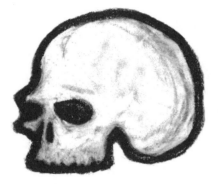

Nagasamala

Trinkets
a pretty skirt
sandalwood fragrance and
a garland—
the cabaret girl
danced for a crowd on main street
while a street band
played
I'd gone into
town with my begging bowl
oh I walked where Mara
       set the snare

Sirivaddha

Streaks of
lightning fall through the cleft
of Vebhara and Pandava—
but within that
cleft through the mountains a son
of the Buddha
keeps vigil

Songs of the Little Hut

The sky god rains
but my hut is well thatch'd
draft-free, simple
I concentrate my mind—
Rain, sky god,
    rain

    —GODHIKA

Who dwells in the little hut?
a solitary hermit
he's shed desire
he keeps a sharp mind
Oh his little hut was not
    built in vain

    —KUTIVIHARIN

You have your old cottage
now you want a new one
but friend don't you realize
a new cottage is just
    new anguish

    —KUTIVIHARIN

The seeing one sees both
the one who sees
and the one who doesn't
The one who doesn't see
sees neither

    —Vappa

My little hut pleases me
I have no need for women
let them take their
fine clothes and trouble
    somewhere else

      —Ramaniyakutika

We dwell alone in the forest
old trees the woodcutter rejected
people look at me
like hell-bound creatures at someone
    going to heaven

    —Vajjiputta

Sivaka Speaks

I hunted the house builder, life after life,
scouring this world and others—
now I've discovered
the house is impermanent.
"You will not build another structure,
the rafters are broken
        the roof collapsed
This mind has been blown asunder—"

The Monk Cittaka

Blue-throated
peacocks
cry through the mist of Karamvi Forest
they wake the drowsing
hermit

Khandasumana Remembers

Khandasumana means "jasmine"—they named him that because jasmine bloomed the day he was born. Hearing the Buddha's teachings, Khandasumana recalled his former births, how he'd offered a sprig of jasmine aeons ago to Kassapa Buddha, though all plucked flowers belonged by decree to the king.

> Merit from one flower
> given to Buddha
> brought me eighty *kotis** of years in heaven—
> with what's left over
> I extinguish delusion

*One *koti* equals ten million.

Anupama

This mind
fierce with desire, chases shadows
chases phantoms
It sets up its own chopping block
I call you witch mind!
Thief mind!
How often does a Buddha appear?
Don't distract me
from the goal!

Rajadatta, the Merchant

When Rajadatta was still young, a group of investors staked him to five hundred carts of merchandise. He took the carts to the city of Rajagaha. There he met a beautiful prostitute whose body so intoxicated him that he lavished 1,000 rupees a day on her. Before he could shake himself free, he'd squandered the whole caravan and ended up penniless. He took to wandering and one day joined a crowd of laymen who'd gone to hear the Buddha speak. Sitting at the edge of the assembly, he listened with deep concentration. The words rang so true and forcefully in his ears that he joined the assembly of monks that day. And recognizing his weakness for women, he took to a charnel ground to practice austerities.

Meanwhile, another caravan leader was also spending thousands on the same prostitute. This man wore a lavishly wrought ring on his hand that the woman coveted fiercely. She hired some men to steal it for her. However, the police were tipped off and raided her house, found the wealthy merchant's ring, killed the prostitute on the spot, and flung her body into the charnel ground.

Rajadatta, tramping about in search of a suitably foul object to meditate on, stumbled across her corpse. "This will do," he thought, and began to brood on impermanence. But those parts of the prostitute no dog or jackal had mangled yet distracted him, and with horror he found himself terribly aroused. Aghast at his fantasies he fled to a safe distance. There, sinking deeply into *dhyana*, with a supreme effort of will he achieved insight. This is his poem:

> A recluse
> went to the burning ground
> found a woman's
> naked corpse
> inside it a tangle of worms
> Others blanched
> and turned away at the sight
> but that poor dead creature's golden
> breasts and
> unshaved cunt
> haunted me until I lost
> control and shuddered with
> violent urges
>
> Quicker than boiling rice
> overflows the pot
> I fled the graveyard
> fled that poor dead creature
> fled until I reached
> a safe secluded spot
> to sit

and cross my legs and
calm my mind

I considered
the object
considered the hungry ignorant acts
that brought it where it lay
considered the tangle of worms
and corpses
I stared into countless
rounds of suffering
stared into greed and hunger
stared on vanity
stared until desire
blinked like a lamp
and went out
Lust no longer assailed me
I made wisdom my own then
yes I accomplished
what had
to be done

Kassapa the Great

I came down from my
mountain hut
into the streets one day
to beg food

I stopped where a leper
was feeding himself
With his rotted leper's hand
into my bowl
he threw a scrap

into my bowl as he
threw it
one of his fingers broke and also fell
I simply leaned against a wall
and ate

Taking whatever scraps
are tossed
finding medicine
in cow dung

sleeping
beneath a tree and wrapped in
tattered robes—

only a man like that
walks free in all the four
directions

only a man like that
walks free

Usabha

Towering clouds
sweep the ridge
The trees grow thick
Ah, excellent
for Usabha
who has a taste for solitude
and forests

Bharata Speaks

Come, Nandaka,
let's give the lion's roar
face to face with all buddhas
We have done it
what the wakeful sage
spurred us on to—
we've shattered the manacles

Sona Potiriyaputta

Night
with its garland of stars
is not for sleeping
The wise sit through it awake
Better an elephant
on the battlefield trample me
than I fall into
hostile hands

Kankha-Revata

A campfire at midnight
eats at the
circle of darkness
subduing the shadows for all
who pass

Even so are the Tathagata's words—

Songs of the
Daughters of Buddha

Citta Speaks

Heaping up good karma in rebirth after rebirth, Citta
had been born a fairy in the ninety-fourth aeon.

> Although I'm thin and weak
> Spring in my once lively gait gone—gone—
> I've climbed the mountain
> leaning on my walking stick
> I throw the cloak off my shoulder
> Overturn the little begging bowl
> Against this rock I lean
> and prop the self of me
> Break through the gloom
> that boxed me in *Ahhhhh*

Addhakasi

I was a prostitute with fees as large
as the whole Kingdom of Kasi
The sheriff fixed it: I was priceless
Then I got disgusted with my figure
No one was interested in it anymore
Used up, tired, weary—this old body,
good for sex, this sex-money body
Where does it go?
How far does it go?
Never again, chasing rebirth after
      rebirth after rebirth

Uppalavanna

Uppalavanna was stunning. She had skin the color of the heart of the blue lotus. "Give us your daughter," everyone begged of her father. But Uppalavanna renounced the world. She repeated some verses she'd heard:

> My daughter
> and I
> married the same man!
> O horror
> It's unnatural
> My hair stands on end
> Sensual desire is
> a thick
> and thorny jungle

She is visited and challenged by Mara in a *sal*-tree grove.

> *Mara:*
> Such beauty is
> vulnerable in
> this fragrant grove
> Foolish girl—
> aren't you afraid of
> being raped?

Uppalavanna:
Were there
a thousand rapists
No hair of mine
would stiffen or tremble
What can you do to me?
I've got the same magic you do, Mara
I can disappear into your body
Look!
I'm standing
between your eyebrows
and you can't see me

Mutta Speaks

Get free, Mutta
free as the moon
free from Rahu the Dragon's claws
mind free, free of debt
heart free
enjoy the food they give you
when you're out begging

Another Mutta

I'm free. Ecstatically free
I'm free from three crooked things:
the mortar
the pestle
and my hunchbacked husband
All that drags me back is cut—cut!

Sumangala's Mother

Sumangala's mother was the wife of a weaver of straw hats.

I'm free
Free from kitchen drudgery
No longer a slave among my dirty cooking pots
(My pot smelled like an old water snake)
And I'm through with my brutal husband
And his tiresome sunshades
I purge lust with a sizzling sound—*pop*
"O happiness," meditate upon
this as happiness

Vimala, the Former Courtesan

Born at Vesali, daughter of a prostitute, Vimala one day spotted Maha-Moggallana going about the town for alms. He was one of the Buddha's most highly realized disciples. She followed, trying to seduce him. Some say she was spurred on by "sectarians." After the elder rebuked her, she felt shame and became a lay believer. She made this confession after joining the order:

> I used to be puffed up
> high on good looks
> intoxicated by a rosy complexion
> voluptuous figure
> I was haughty, vain,
> looked down on other women
> I was young
> All painted up
> I stood at the brothel door
> like a hunter laying snares,
> showing my wares—
> Here are my breasts, a thigh
> *(lifts a skirt)*
> I conjured, mocked, seduced—
> Today I'm bald

Clad in the outer robe, I go begging
Sitting at the foot of a tree,
I no longer discriminate
All ties have been cut
I said, cut

Ambapali Speaks

Ambapali's life was the stuff of legend, and an interesting twist of karma. In a former life she was a *bhikkhuni*, or nun. She had observed another nun spit in front of a shrine and rebuked her, saying, "What prostitute has been spitting in this place?" Ambapali, whose name means "mango protectress" or "mango guardian," came to birth spontaneously at the foot of a mango tree in the city of Vesali. She was extraordinarily beautiful, and princes fought fiercely over her. To end the contention it was soon decided that she be made the chief courtesan of the city. Prosperity graced Vesali, it is said, because of her notoriety. She had a son by King Bimbisara, who later became a Buddhist monk (the elder Vimal-Kondanna). Eventually abandoning fame and wealth to seek the Dharma, according to legend she entertained the Buddha with a retinue of monks, who had been warned by Gautama not to lose their heads over her. Later, out of strong devotion, she built a hermitage, or *vihara*, on her land and gave it to the Buddha. He rested there in his eightieth year, four months before he died.

> Once my hair was black like the color of bees
> > alive—curly
> Now it is dry like bark fibers of hemp

I'm getting old
This is true, I tell you the truth

Covered with flowers, my head was fragrant
        as a perfumed box
Now, because of old age, it smells like dog's fur

Thick like a grove it used to be beautiful—
        ends parted by comb and pin
Now it's thin, I'm telling the truth

This was a head with fine pins once,
        decorated with gold, plaited, so beautiful
Now bald

My eyebrows were like crescents
        exquisitely painted by artists
Now because of old age they droop down with
                wrinkles
Ah, I'm telling the truth

My eyes used to be shiny, brilliant as jewels
Now they don't look so good

My nose was like a delicate peak
Now it's a long pepper
This scarecrow is telling the truth

My earlobes—can you believe it?
     were like well-fashioned bracelets
Now they're heavy with creases

My teeth were pearly white
     like the bud of a plantain
Now they're broken and yellow
Indeed, this is the truth

Sweet was my singing like the cuckoo in the grove
Now my voice cracks and falters
Hear it? These words are true

My neck used to be soft like a well-rubbed
     conch shell
Now it bends, broken

My arms were round like crossbars
Now they're weak as the *petali* tree

My hands were gorgeous—they used to be,
     used to be gorgeous—
Covered with signet rings, decorated with gold
Now they are like onions and radishes
This is true, I tell you

My breasts looked great—
     round, swelling, close together, lofty
Now they hang down like waterless water bags

My body used to be shiny as a sheet of gold
Now it is covered with very fine wrinkles

Both thighs—and this was once considered a
          compliment—
        looked like elephants' trunks—very interesting
I swear I'm telling the truth
Now they're like stalks of bamboo

My calves too, like stalks of sesame

My feet used to be elegant
        like shoes of soft cotton wool
Now they are cracked and wrinkled
This hag speaks true

I had the body of a queen
Now it's lowly, decrepit, an old house
Plaster falling off
Sad, but true

Patacara Speaks

Patacara lost a husband to a snakebite, an infant to a hawk, another child to drowning, parents and a brother to calamity.

> Young brahmins plough fields,
> sow seeds,
> nourish their wives and children,
> get wealthy
> Why can't I find peace?
> I'm virtuous
> comply with the teacher
> not lazy or puffed up
>
> One day washing my feet
> I watched the water as it
> trickled down the slope
> I fixed my mind
> the way you'd
> train a thoroughbred horse
>
> Later, taking my lamp
> I enter my cell
> sit on my bed and
> watch the flame
> I extinguish the wick

with a needle
The release of my mind
is like the quenching of the lamp
O the nirvana of the little lamp!

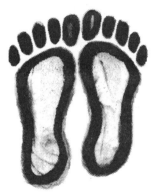

Sangha Speaks

Home I've left
Child I've left
Cherished herds—far behind
Lust—even lust—left
Left ill will too
Gone ignorance
Ignorance back off
I'm safe without you

Tissa

Tissa,
Get with it
Don't let "it"
pass you by
Those who miss "it"
grieve
when they're
stuck in hell
Practice! Practice!

Punnika, the Slave

Still prideful after numerous auspicious births, Punnika was reborn a slave at Savatthi, in the household of Anathapindika, the treasurer. She won her master's esteem after turning an *udakasuddhika* (baptist brahmin) to the Dharma. Her master freed her and consented that she enter the Order of Nuns.

> *Punnika:*
> I'm a water carrier, slave
>   to my mistress' anger
> Bitter winter:
> I'm down
> by the freezing Achiravati
>   drawing water
> But what frightens you, Brahmin?
> What makes you go to the river
> Your limbs are shaking from the cold

> *Udakasuddhika:*
> Don't you know, Punnika?
> I'm performing this ablution to prevent evil
>   Whoever commits evil
>   *is* saved by washing in water

Punnika:
Whoever told you
washing frees you from evil karma?
Ridiculous!
Superstition!
The blind leading the blind!
If that were true
fish and turtles would swim in heaven
along with frogs,
water snakes, crocodiles
Sheep butchers, pork butchers,
fishermen,
animal trappers,
thieves, executioners
all free from bad karma
after splashing themselves with water?
(Not to mention all kinds of
other despicable rogues)
If these streams carried away evil
they would carry away your virtue too
You would be devoid of both
O Brahmin, give it up
don't go to the water out of ignorance
Spare your skin the icy cold!

Ubbiri's Lament

Ubbiri was born in this Buddha-era at Savatthi to the family of an eminent burgess. Extremely beautiful, she was brought to the house of the king of Kosala, Pasenedi himself. A few years later she gave birth to a daughter named Jiva ("alive"), and the king anointed her queen. Soon after, the little girl died and the mother, out of her mind with grief, went daily to the charnel ground. She tried to worship the Buddha but gave up, so obsessed she was by her loss, and went lamenting to the river Achiravati. Buddha revealed himself to her:

Buddha:
O Ubbiri who howls for her dead daughter
"Jiva, Jiva, come back!"
come to your senses
Eighty-four thousand daughters with the name "Jiva"
have been burned in this charnel ground.
Which "Jiva" do you mourn?
Which of the countless "Jivas" do you mourn?

Ubbiri then spoke:
The master plucks the fiery dart
from my heart
It was rooted deep in there,

My loss—O Jiva!—became my obsession
Today I've stopped craving her
I let Jiva go
I take refuge in the Buddha
the Dharma, the Sangha

Siha

She thought of suicide, but gave it up, singing:

> Distracted
> too passionate
> dumb about
> the way things work
> I was stung and tossed
> by memories
> Haunted, you could say
> I went on like this,
> wandering for seven years
> Thin, pale, desperate
> Nothing to hold me
> Taking a rope
> I went to the woods
> *Hanging is better*
> *than this low life*
> The noose was strong
> I tied it to the branch of a tree
> flung it 'round my neck
> when suddenly—look—
> it snapped!
> Not my neck
> my *heart* was free

Vasitthi

Out of my mind
deranged with love of my lost son
Out of my senses
Naked—hair disheveled
I wandered here, there
I lived on rubbish heaps
in a cemetery, on a highway
I wandered three years in hunger and thirst
Then I saw the Buddha
gone to Mithila
I paid homage
He pitied me
and taught me the Dharma
I went forth into the homeless state

Kisa-Gotami and the Mustard Seed

Born into a poor family, Kisa-Gotami was named "Lean Gotami" because of the frailness of her body; when she married, they chided her as "nobody's daughter." When she bore a son, they finally paid her respect. But the boy died young—he'd just turned old enough to run and play—and Kisa went insane with grief. A wild thought came to her: *They will try to take my child and expose him.* So she lifted his corpse upon her hip and went from door to door, begging "give me medicine for my child!" "Medicine? (crazy woman) What for?" was the response. She was out of touch. Someone finally took pity and sent her to the Buddha. He glimpsed the promise in her and instructed, "Go, go, enter the town, and collect a little mustard seed from any house where no one has died." She went from house to house, but at each one someone had died. The truth dawned: *This will be the situation in the whole town.* She finally sought a charnel ground to place her dead child in, murmuring:

> No village "law,"
> > no city law merely
> No law for this clan or
> > that one alone
> For the whole world, for the gods even

> *All is impermanent*
> > this is the Truth

"Gotami, did you collect the mustard seed?" the Buddha asked. Gotami answered, "This is the work of the little mustard seed," and requested ordination. She was proclaimed first among wearers of the rough raiment.

Reflecting later, she sang:

> Excellent to have wise, noble friends
> One should know a few things
> It helps your pain
> But one should understand how pain arises
> > how it ceases
> (the Eightfold Path, the Four Noble Truths)
> Mark the sorrow, mark how it comes
> Being a woman is painful
> Miserable sharing a home with hostile wives
> Miserable giving birth in bitter pain
> Some cut their own throats
> More squeamish women take poison
> I saw—like others—my husband die
> Two sons dead
> and mother, father, brother
> cremated on the funeral pyre
> Miserable, a whole family destroyed!

Tears shed for a thousand lifetimes
Watched my babe's flesh devoured by
        dogs, jackals, and tigers
            in the charnel ground
But I survived
quenched desire
Saw the teachings as a mirror
        held up to show me my crazy mind
Now healed
The poison darts extracted from my heart
All this done and
done by me

The *theri* Kisa-Gotami
saw herself in the mirror
and witnessed these things

Nanduttara

I used to worship
fire, the moon, sun,
all the gods
I used to go down
to the riverbanks
for the bathing rites
I took holy vows
shaved half my head
slept on the ground
wouldn't eat food after sundown
Then I decked myself
out with many ornaments
baths, unguents, massage—
you name it—
Tried everything
to stave off death
I was a slave to my body
Then I really "got" it
saw my body as it really is
went homeless
Lust? Sex?
Forget it
All that binds me head and foot
is loosened

Subha Speaks: Moon as Toy

After heaping up lifetimes of merit under former buddhas, Subha, whose name literally means "bright" or "shining," was born in this Buddha-era in Rajagaha to a prestigious brahmin family. Eschewing marriage, she became a nun under the teacher Prajapati. In keeping with the Buddha's *nissayas,* or guidelines, for monastic living, Subha took to heart the admonition to dwell at the foot of a tree. She loved to wander in the forest. But this was before a nun was raped in the woods and the rules drastically changed. The *Cullavagga* states: "Now at that time, nuns dwelt in the forest and wayward men violated them. They told this to the Buddha. He replied, 'A nun is not to adopt a forest life.'"

A young man tried to seduce the *bhikkhuni* Subha as she was entering Jivaka's tantalizing mango grove:

She:
Why do you stop me—
What have I done to you?
It's not right to proposition a nun.
I've been trained in the precepts, you not.
I'm pure, you're impure.
On top of that you're obnoxious. Out of my way!

He:

But you're young and beautiful. Cast off that silly
   yellow robe and let's make love in this wood.

Blossoms smell sweet from the tall trees. Spring is a
   happy season. Let's make love in this flowering
   wood.

The trees cry out when shaken by wind. It's wonderful
   and frightening.

What fun can you have alone in the wood?

You could get lost.

The forest is haunted—you want to go it alone?

Haunted by wild beasts—rutting, savage elephants.

You could go about a forest like this like a gold idol.
   Just be my little doll. You'd have beautiful clothes.
   I'd be your slave. First let's lie in the grove together.
   O Kinnari, elf of the forest with languid eyes. Do
   as I say, please. I'll make you happy. Come live in
   my house. You'll live in a palace of verandas and
   terraces with women attending you. You'll wear the
   finest muslin from Banares, cover yourself with
   garlands, creams. I'll give you ornaments of precious
   stones, gold work, pearls, anything you want! Come
   lie on a bed with a clean cover, spread with a fine
   woolen blanket—quite new, extremely costly—
   decorated with sandalwood, having an excellent
   smell. Come.

(He says almost to himself):

A blue lotus rises up with gorgeous blossoms, preyed on
by water sprites. Great! No other man has ever touched
her.

She:

What seems to infatuate you so much? Me? In this
carrion-filled body of mine? Look again. What
makes you speak like this?

He:

It's your eyes like a gazelle, like the elf. Your eyes make
me wild. They're like buds of a lotus, spotless as
gold. I'm crazy with desire for you! Even if you go
away I'll never forget your miracle eyes. And long
lashes. Pure gaze. No eyes are dearer to me.

(He lunges for her.) She:

You're crazy! You're on the wrong track. You want the
moon as a toy. You want to jump over Mount Meru.
You want the impossible. You're trying to seduce a
child of the Buddha. I desire no one now. No lust
for any man. Desire has been scattered like sparks
from burning coal. It's poison, forget it. No lust for
any man. Can't see him. I've slain the root and
branch of lust through following the Noble Path.
Tempt someone else if you can, forget Subha who
doesn't see any man. I'm awake in the midst of
praise, blame, pain, pleasure. All composite oppo-

sites, all conditioned things are disgusting. I tell
you, my mind doesn't cling to anything at all. The
darts are extracted from my heart, wounds healed,
no more intoxicants. I've seen puppets and dolls
fastened by strings and sticks, made to dance in
crazy ways. Once the strings and sticks are removed,
then what? Once they're thrown away, mutilated,
scattered, lost, broken to bits, then what?
This little body, this phantom body, does not exist.
A puppet can't exist without sticks and strings. If
something does not exist without phenomena, on
what can you fix your mind? You see a picture on a
wall smeared with yellow ointment—is that it?
You're confused, you mistake the image for the
thing itself. O Blind One! I tell you, you run after
an empty thing—a mirage, a golden tree at the end
of a dream, a puppet show in the middle of a
crowd. Delusion, conjurer's trick! Forget it. An eye is
a ball set in a hollow with a bubble in the middle,
briny tears, it secretes slime too. Here, look at this!

*(The young maiden plucks out her eye to give to her seducer.
She is unattached. She has a calm mind.)*

He:
Agh!

*(He's horrified. His passion dies on the spot. He begs
forgiveness.)*

Please put it back! Become whole! Forgive me, I won't
trouble you again. Please put your sight back. You
pierce me, all right. I embraced fire. I seized a poiso-
nous snake. I beg you, please put your eye back!

The nun then visited the excellent Buddha. And on seeing her virtue the Buddha restored her eye.

Sukka

Sukka was a great preacher, attended by five hundred *bhikkhunis*. One day after begging alms in Rajagaha, Sukka returned to the nuns' settlement and began to teach "with a great company seated around her." Her words were so powerful and sweet (like mead and ambrosia) that they inspired a tree spirit (*devata*) that stood at the end of the Sisters' terrace to get up and walk the roads and squares proclaiming Sukka's excellence.

The spirit of the tree walking the streets of the city speaks:

> What's wrong with you men
> of Rajagaha?
> You're acting drunk, stupid, lazy
> Don't you want to hear the woman Sukka
> teach the precious Dharma?
>
> The wise drink it up
> it's irresistible, quenching
> An inexhaustible elixir she pours into you
>
> Her words are sweet
> Travelers drink them like rain

And hearing what the tree spirit said, people were excited and flocked to Sukka. At the end of her life, Sukka declared her realization:

I'm named Sukka because I am a "child of light."
I subjugated desire, focused my mind
Conquered Mara and his tempters
Ah, my little frame breaks
but it's the last body I speak in

The Ballad of Isidasi

In the beautiful kingdom of Pataliputta
named for the fragrant trumpet flower
lived two *bhikkhunis,* born of the Shakya clan—
Isidasi and Bodhi—holy beauties
who delighted in their study and practice
They were erudite,
accomplished meditators

Listen how
after having made the round for alms,
eaten, and washed their little begging bowls
they cheerfully sat down
on a secluded bank
by the great river Ganges
and began to speak together
What on earth brought you to renunciation
Isidasi?
You're lovely to look at—
such noble carriage
still young
Were you sick of the domestic life,
Was that it?
Are you really going to stay a nun forever?

And in this quiet spot by the river
Isidasi—now
skilled in the Dharma
now strong in the Dharma,
took up her long strange tale:

Listen, Bodhi, listen to me
I'll tell you how I became a nun

My father was a merchant, a model citizen
of Ujjeni—Avanti's most excellent city
I was his only daughter—his delight—
prized jewel of his eye

One day a high nobleman arrived from Saketa
laden with exotic treasure
sent by a rich merchant
to woo me for his son

My father gave me willingly
No protest. No bargaining

I tell you I waited on my in-laws day and night
bowed and scraped
Paid endless homage,
bowing, obsessively prostrating at their feet
Waited on all my husband's kin
brothers, sisters, his whole retinue in fact
Did everything I was supposed to—everything!

Leapt up,
gave my seat to them zealously
as they'd enter the room
Timid, really overdoing it
Constantly serving drink and food
catering to every need

Bolt up early, Isidasi, wake up
Wash your hands and feet
Now go to him like a good wife
Cup your hands obediently

I'd arrive with soap, combs, ornaments,
dress and groom him as if I were
a slave girl, he the king

I'd boil the rice gruel
wash the pots and pans
Looking after him the way
a mother does her only son

He disliked me from the start
Why? Why?
I who'd shown such slavish devotion
up before dawn, industrious,
humble
I who'd shown real affection
I'd reach for him . . .

One day he said to his parents:
I can't live with Isidasi anymore!
—just like that—
I won't live with her
Give me permission to go

What's wrong with you son?
Isidasi is clever,
a diligent housewife
gets up early, does the chores
How can you say this?
What's happened?
Why doesn't she please you?

She's done no harm
I just can't stand to be around her
She disgusts me
She drives me away

What offense did you commit, Isidasi?
They turned to me . . .

Nothing, I protested—
I've done nothing—
Never said an evil word
Never hurt my husband
What can I do when he loathes me so?

I was devastated
They led me back to my father's home
We've lost a beautiful goddess, they said
to keep our son at home

Then my father gave me to the household
of a second rich man of noble family
for half the bride price
I lived there a month till he too
rejected me
and I'd served him like the other—
like a slave

My father runs out in the street
like a crazy person
and grabs the first mendicant he sees
Come be my son-in-law!
Throw away that ragged robe and begging pot!

But the *sadhu* having lived with me two weeks
demanded
Give me back my cup and robe
I want to go back to the homeless life
beg for scraps out in the street

What hasn't been done for you here
Tell us quickly what we can do for you!
(my father was scared to lose him too)

Even if I were honored like royalty
I tell you I simply couldn't be
under the same roof with Isidasi!

I was alone again
I wanted to die
O please let me die or just
let me go off a wanderer, I pleaded

Then the noble lady Jinadatta
a learned practitioner
—it was most auspicious—
arrived at the house
on her daily round for alms

and as she entered
I offered her my seat
then bent over
paying homage at her feet

I gave her food and drink
And after she was satisfied
I blurted out
O Noble Lady, I wish to go forth
I want to renounce the world
Take me with you

No, no

Stay here,
practice here!—my father broke in
You can take care of the ascetics
and brahmins from here—please stay

But I was wailing now
weeping, begging
praying to him to let me go
I must wear out my evil karma
Let me go

He finally relented with his blessing
Go get enlightened Isidasi
Attain nibbana, little unfortunate one

And I said good-bye to my parents
good-bye to tribal kin
and seven days after my renunciation
I gained the three knowledges

Now I know my last seven births
I understand now, Bodhi
Listen well to my tale

I was a goldsmith in the city of Erakaccha
Wealthy, handsome, lusty
So intoxicated by my own youth and prowess
I slept with other mens' wives

For these indiscretions
I cooked in hell a long time
till I found rebirth in the body of an ape
Only alive seven days
Dog-Ape, the monkeys' chief
castrated me
Castrated me when I was only seven days old
Was this the result of my former lust?

Fallen from there,
having died in the Sindhava Forest
I was born the offspring of
a one-eyed lame she-goat
Again castrated,
carrying children on my back twelve years
I was worm-eaten, tailless, pathetic

Down again
O fallen from there
I was reborn a lac-red bull belonging
to a cattle dealer
castrated another time
pulling a huge plough
blind, no tail, sorry sight
All because I seduced another man's wife?

Next: hermaphrodite
born in the street to a poor household slave

all my miserable life neither man nor woman
and died after thirty years, woe woe

Another time back, daughter now
to a poor carter's family, father oppressed
with debts to usurers
and he used me to pay off the debt
owed to a shrewd caravan merchant
The man dragged me off—
weeping and wailing from my home

When I turned sixteen the merchant's son Giridasa
who loved me, made me his wife
But he had a second wife he loved too and
she was good
And I brought no harmony to that house

See now, Bodhi, how the karma ripened
from this last life and how
it manifested
though I waited on them—all of them
and was their humble slave

Look at my births, observe well, Sister Bodhi:
Sex-craving idiot, helpless monkey babe,
pathetic beasts of burden—goat made ragged by
labor, no eyes in this cow's head—
unspeakable life as hermaphrodite—

was I man or woman?—begging in the streets
then wretched wife, unloved
scorned wife again, again, again—enough!

Well—that's all at an end now
Ah (she lets out a cheerful sigh)
that's all finished now, done
I say *done*

An Anonymous Sister Speaks

It's been twenty-five years since I became a nun
But I'm still restless
No peace of mind—not even one moment
(she snaps her fingers)
Every thought's of sex
I hold out my arms
Cry out like a madwoman
Then I go into my cell
But I heard Dhamma-Dinna preach
and she taught me impermanence
I sat down to meditate:
I know I've lived before
My celestial eye has been purified
I see I see other lives past and present
I read other minds present and past
The ear element is purified
I hear I hear I can really hear

Dantika (Little Tamed Woman)

As I came out from napping
on Vulture's Peak
an elephant swayed up onto the riverbank
after its bath
A man taking a goad commanded
"Give me your foot"
and the elephant obeyed
It stretched its foot
and the man sprang to the elephant's neck
I saw the untamed mind
I saw the elephant bend to the master's will
I went deep into the forest
and contemplated these things

Bhadda Kundalakesa: Called
The Curly Haired, the Ex-Jain

For many aeons Bhadda heaped up merit, experienced rebirth after rebirth among gods and men, and even lived royally as one of the seven daughters of Kiki, king of Kasi. She kept the precepts twenty-thousand years. Born in this Buddha-era in Rajagaha, daughter of the king's treasurer, Bhadda was reared in luxury. She saw Satthuka, a highway robber, being led to his execution. She swooned to her couch, trembling: "If I get him I'll live; if not, I die." Her doting father bribed the guard to release Satthuka, ordered him bathed with scented water, then had him brought to Bhadda, who was—as usual—wearing her magnificent jewels. Satthuka coveted the jewels—he couldn't help it, he was a thief to the core. "O Bhadda, when the guards took me to Robber's Cliff, I vowed to the *lokapala* that I would make an offering if my life were spared. Make one ready for me." She desperately wanted to please him and mounted the chariot and drove to Robber's Cliff. Satthuka dismissed Bhadda's attendants and took her alone to the summit. He was abrupt with her, surly, spoke no words of affection. She was suddenly suspicious and guessed his plot. Lucky Bhadda! He ordered her to take off her outer robe and wrap her jewels in it.

"What have I done wrong?" she asked. "You fool, do you think I've come all this way to make an offering? I've brought you here to steal your jewels!" "But, beloved," she said persuasively, "whose are the ornaments and whose am I? Grant me this one wish: let me embrace you wearing my jewels." The clever girl embraced him in front and then, as if hugging him from behind, pushed him over the cliff! The cliff deity saw her do this and praised her cunning:

> Woman may prove as clever as Man
> when she's quick to see

Realizing she could never return home after these disastrous events, Bhadda decided to "leave the world" and joined the Order of the Niganthas. And when they asked, "In what grade do you make your renunciation?" she requested the most extreme: "Whatever that is, perform it on me." So they tore out her hair with a palmyra comb. (When her hair grew back in tight curls, they called her The Curly Haired.) But she soon exhausted her practice and study with the Jains, saying there was nothing distinctive in it, that she'd gone as far as she could go. Seeking out more learned persons, she acquired further knowledge and skills, so that eventually none could equal her in debate. Prodigious Bhadda! She'd place a heap of sand at the gate of some village or town and stick a rose-apple branch in it, saying,

"Whoever challenges me to debate, let him trample this bough." She told the children to watch for a challenger, but none came. She'd move on.

Then she set up her branch at the gate of Savatthi when the Buddha was nearby, dwelling with his disciples in the Jeta Wood. Sariputta—the most accomplished of the Buddha's followers—entered the city alone and, seeing Bhadda's rose-apple signal, wished to tame her. He instructed the children to trample on the bough. "Who's done this?" Hearing it was the accomplished elder, she went about the town excitedly gathering followers to come see her with the Shakyan recluse. She found Sariputta seated beneath a tree, and after friendly greetings they began their debate, she asking all the questions. He answered them all, and after exhausting her mind she fell silent. "I'll ask but one question," he said. "Ask it," she replied. "One—what is that?" ("*Ekan nama kin?*") She didn't get the point of this; her mind was dark. He said, "You know not this much! How can you know anything else?"* He taught her the

---

*"What is that which is named one?" is the literal translation of Sariputta's question. Did Bhadda lack a ready reply because the question seemed so vague? The oldest *Upanishads* give many answers along the lines of "All things become one in *prajna*" or "In the beginning there was One only." Bhadda may have known this monism, but as a sincere Jain she rejected it. Jainism, like Buddhism, is not monistically or pantheistically inclined. In the *Khuddakapatha*, an ancient catechism, the question occurs, but the answer is, "All beings are sustained by food." Hence, as Caroline

Norm and she fell at his feet to take refuge. "No, no, go for refuge to the Exalted One" and she did and the Buddha, seeing the depth of her knowledge, said:

> She speaks better than a thousand verses
> One stanza brings peace and calm

As the Buddha spoke she attained arhatship, and going to her Sisters' quarters, she sang:

> Bald, dirty, half naked
> I was ignorant of how things work
> Thought harmless things held harm
> or the other way around
> Then I went to hear the Buddha
> and knelt at his feet
> "Come Bhadda," he said
> and that was my ordination
>
> I've been a pilgrim over fifty years
> In Anga, Magadha and in Vajji
> In Kasi also, and the land of Kosala
> living on people's alms
> A layman gave Bhadda a robe
> and she found herself

Rhys Davids notes, Sariputta's meaning presumably was, "State any one fact for the whole of one class of things." One wonders if Bhadda's blanking out on such a dry, semantic question shows that she actually had the upper hand.

Sisupacala Speaks with Mara

Sisupacala was sure of herself. Her senses pure, her perception clear, she drank life's elixir—a sweet fluid, sustaining, that replenished her mind.

> *Mara interrupts:*
> Don't forget where you've been before,
> those other lives
> you led in bittersweet realm
> —animals, demons,
> *pretas* your friends, companions—
> Think about it, long for it
> *(he whispers in her ear)*
> Yearn again for the Kamaloka and the
> seductive beauty of the dark
> gods who rule in shadow
> and the blissed-out gods
> who rule by day
> They'll take you, caress
> your naked body . . .

> *She:*
> Stop, Mara
> Don't you know those gods
> go from birth to death to birth to
> death again again,

become this, become that,
become this again, become that
You know the Kamaloka
stinks with lust
I tell you the world is blazing, blazing
the whole world's in flames
I tell you it's flared up
the world is shaken
your words are shaken
the whole world's ablaze!

Afterword

"I went to the woods because I wanted to live deliberately," wrote Henry David Thoreau in *Walden*, getting the elemental urge into a few precise words. In this age-old human desire lies the attraction of the poems of the *Theragatha* and *Therigatha*, uttered or sung or whispered 2,500 years ago by the earliest Buddhist practitioners—women and men intent on leading lives marked by deliberation. In every culture that has left behind evidence of itself, one finds people to whom the same old hankering comes: to live simply, resolutely, with minimal possessions of only the most necessary sort. To pass the time in reflection, unharried by the endless round of buying and selling. To live out life on one of those frontiers—spiritual or geographic or both—where philosophy and poetry seem the only languages big enough to accommodate the adventure. This is a book of ancients who went to the woods.

Twenty-five hundred years ago extensive tracts of forest covered parts of northern India, particularly the wide, fertile watershed drained by the river Ganges. In contrast to the open plains and farmlands, where the sun could be blistering, the forests were cool, breezy, and pleasant. Socially, it was a time of massive dissatisfaction. A burgeoning merchant class, drawing on the region's natural resources and trading widely throughout the South Asian subcontinent, had helped build the thronging cities of the Gangetic plain. While cosmopolitan life offered unprecedented opportunity to people relocating to the cities—particularly the freedom found in breaking with the constraints of traditional village life—a recognizable urban malaise had set in. It was the old problem of an expanding economy and the confusion of values that comes with it. The traditional *varna-ashrama* system of Brahminism, founded on caste hierarchies and rigid expectations regarding an individual's duties throughout life, had a stink of antiquity and irrelevance to it. And religion, dominated by imperious priests who demanded cattle for presiding over births, weddings, initiations, and funerals, was in many sectors seen as just a dry rattling—empty, formulaic, and devoid of spiritual substance. Where could one go for nourishment?

And so there occurred one of those considerable, deliberate migrations out and away from the cities. Not just the elderly were freeing themselves from encrusted social demands (India's law books had always sanctioned a spiritual departure into the forests for those who had seen "the eyes of their children's children"), but the young and intellectually hungry were heading out also, heading toward woodland and grove, to live as wanderers and seekers. This is the period (circa 800–400 BCE) of the venerable teachers of the *Upanishads*—contemplatives and thinkers who practiced yoga and sagely discussed metaphysics with students who clustered around them, "fuel in hand" (so the documents describe them, meaning students brought traditional offerings, not currency or cattle but simply food and a bit of firewood). By the hundreds such students sat sharpening their wits in debate or undertaking austerities in forest groves.

Several figures who crop up in accounts of Shakyamuni Buddha's life are renowned teachers and sages of the times, familiar to the annals of Vedanta or Jainism. Young Siddhartha Gautama, a prince who had fled his ancestral home to solve the mysteries of old age, sickness, and death, learned a thing or two from some of these philosophers. The future Buddha was by no means a solitary seeker. He lived in one of those consequential periods in history when yogins, wanderers, teachers, hungry-eyed students, cult founders, and Paracletes meet under the trees, swapping philosophies and poems.

Poems? Yes, something close. A great many passages in the old holy books of India are poetry of a refined and elegant order. Poets, as always, took part in this exhilarating revolution in consciousness. When Prince Siddhartha—called Buddha or "Wakened One" by his admirers after he had opened his wisdom eye—began to attract students, he drew to his side a number of poets and scholars who had already acquired reputations. He also drew unsophisticated, illiterate, low-caste folk—who were nonetheless quite capable of setting their personal observation to metric patterns they knew from village folk songs. With varying degrees of skill, many of the Buddha's students elaborated their personal insights into verse form. They followed his injunction, moreover, to refrain from isolating themselves within the formidable Sanskrit language, a sacred tongue jealously guarded at that time by caste-conscious priests, who would let no woman, child, or laborer converse in it. The Buddha's students, leading the old life of the wanderer, transmitted their insights in the local language. And so they set forth through the forests to talk shop in Magadhi, a far-flung dialect of the region they wandered.

The books that collect the verse of these early renunciants are called *Theragatha* and *Therigatha*—songs (*gatha*) of the *thera* and *theri*, or "monks and nuns," as scholars often call them. But *thera* and its feminine form *theri* mean simply "elder"—a term applied to senior disciples of the Buddha. These disciples lived on the road, ranging from town to town, governed by a fierce set of rules and sleeping in forests or city parks. Only temporarily did they settle in, knocking the road dust off their feet in little out-of-the-way retreats—caves or woodland huts—during the rainy season when travel was difficult. Monasteries as permanent residences did not exist until hundreds of years later. So it is accurate to think of these folk as itinerant monks and nuns of highway and forest, not of the cloister.

Elsewhere, these disciples have been referred to as sons and daughters of the Buddha. It is a tender expression, suggesting the relationships that bound them. They pursued very austere lives indeed—carrying no articles but a robe and a needle to patch it, a begging bowl, and a razor to shave the head. They probably chanted their poetry, keeping snatches of it alive to bring inspiration to the duller moments of their lives. As they kept no musical instruments, each recitation was probably a rather sober, restrained performance.

Kept alive orally for hundreds of years, the poems were finally transcribed along with the rest of the Buddhist canon onto long strips of prepared palm leaf, into the dialect known as Pali, at a historic council of scholars in Sri Lanka, during the reign of King Vattagamani (circa 89–77 BCE). An earlier scholar, Dhammapala (call him an anthologist), had arranged the old poems—the better to memorize them—in an order rather artificially based on length: two-line Imagist-type poems first, then three-line poems, four-line poems, and so forth, up to the formidable balladlike narratives.

Dhammapala also formalized the prose anecdotes in which some of the verses lie set like little gems. These compilations of folktales recount what you might need to know of the poet's life or the occasion that fired the verse. Without these narratives many of the poems would be nearly incomprehensible. Most of the stories detail the poet's first encounter with the Buddha or, in the case of the women in particular, with some senior disciple. Whether these folk actually studied with the Buddha, or whether the accounts of their lives are embellishments a band of storytellers threw around the songs, nobody knows for sure—it is common for oral anecdote to collect wherever archaic and cryptic verse forms occur. But the poets did know the Buddha's teaching. Knew how to put it into practice. Many poems end with the refrain, "Done is Buddha's bidding" (*katam buddhassa sasananti*).

Tradition holds the poems themselves to be canonical (authentic holy utterance). Accounts of the poets' lives in prose are not. Yet both serve us well. The stories are vivid, hair-raising, funny, pointed. The verse involves no posturing—is never a big deal, never inflated, just an ordinary way to talk about crisply experienced moments of life.

When recounting incidents of their lives, these ancients showed a sharp eye for detail. Part of the poignancy arises from their fear of enslavement by family or society (ancient India had a strictly exacting and claustrophobic structure of caste, family, and clan allegiances) or by all the ordinary anxieties and tragedies: death, poverty, violence, loss of parents or children. For the men, hopeless work in the fields or at menial tasks, or the uncertain business of buying and selling with its ever-present specter of bankruptcy. For the women, marriage, grueling housework, and submission to child-bearing and village chores, a round of dirty pots and tiresome husbands. A few ladies trying to get past that but forced into prostitution—on the streets or, more luckily, at court (old books euphemistically refer to "court ladies" or "courtesans"). Many finding themselves the prey of seducers and rapists. It is an entirely familiar world.

A few elements at first don't seem so familiar, particularly the poets' attitudes toward the body, the extreme revulsion that again and again fills their songs. One should remember that one of the key early meditations was on the inevitability of death and decay—not simply the body's "leaky sweating" foulness but its terrible impermanence. The requisite practice? To sit watchfully in a graveyard, to observe unsentimentally the baleful end that will come to your own corpse. This practice certainly tempered sexual eagerness and in fact was often recommended as the antidote to a run-amok sensuality. And why were the disciples so fearful of sex? Remember, in their day in northern India, family relations were tight and highly regulated. Sex in most cases meant marriage, unwelcome in-laws, a succession of children some of whom will die. Resentful co-wives. Mouths to feed. Aunts and uncles to entertain, vicious tax collectors to hold at bay. When the monks and nuns recoiled in horror from sexual relations, their reason was not some inexplicable premodern hang-up. They had simply seen past the immediate passion and gazed with unobstructed vision upon the rounds of cause and effect.

The canonical editions of these poems place them in a specific order, as we have noted, from shortest to longest in accordance with the number of verses (*shloka*) each song contains. We have not presented all of the poems but only those (and, occasionally, only those verses of a poem) that strike us as good and felicitous poetry. We have arranged them in an order that is less mechanical, less bookish, trying to get back to the initial excitement each poem thrilled with as it emerged from the unlocked throat of its singer. This set of versions is a poet's book, sparked by the modern excitement of encountering these ancients. An excitement that has gotten a bit tarnished by the poems' being considered holy writ for too long. (If you are interested, look at some of the earlier English-language versions listed in the bibliography.) Mixing up the poems returns them, we hope, to the charmed vitality they enjoyed centuries before they were transcribed by the Sri Lankan scholars—restores the freshness they certainly had when the seekers, struck by wild insight, cried out whatever anguish and solace they had known in their lives.

To a poet, every life is a sacred inscription. It is the

lives of these ancients, the textures of their experience, that grip us: fears, loves, mishaps, expectations, delights. Theirs was one world that appeared and, because of the impermanence of all things, blinked out. Ours is another such sphere, subject also to the simple truth of impermanence, enjoying its bubblelike moment between birth and extinction. We appreciate their dry, unsentimental tone, whether they cocked a skeptical eye at a crane fleeing a thunderhead, watched with panic a corpse flare in the charnel ground, or cast a quiet moment of thought back over lives full of cook pots, demanding relatives, tough chores, and uncertain friendships. A few poets looked remarkably deep into their minds and their poems and conjured former lives—as abused wives, as *pretas* ("ghosts"—not scary creatures, pitiable rather), or as castrated animals; as beggar or cripple, prostitute or hermaphrodite, or simply a succession of birth forms, dropping through womb after womb. Driven by habit: old avarice, cunning, and ignorance.

These folk are hardheaded and hard living, not much interested in the supernatural or in the deceptive intricacies of magic. A few ghosts or preternatural sprites walk into the poems, but these very ordinary creatures are to be neither feared nor envied. They are simply anguished sentient beings, working out the fruit of past actions, caught up in illusory notions—no different from the castrated goat or the flea-bitten dog of another poem.

Only one figure of loathing appears, and he does so with a haunting consistency. It is as though he dwells in the margin of each poem even when not named. This is Mara, the Tempter, whose name means death, or could perhaps more rigorously be translated as *"death-in-life."* He could be a figure from the Old Testament desert or an American corporate meeting-room. He is truly international and speaks everyone's language. Wily, mean-tempered, holding countless means at his disposal, he possesses great wealth and endless rhetorical persuasions. His only aim seems to be to cut a deal at all costs. Time and again he attempts to trade transient and un-possessible things like sex, privilege, or money to lure the poets from the one thing that counts—a life lived deliberately.

Mara appears nowhere in Indian mythology prior to the early Buddhist texts. It is as though the invigorating thought of the elder poets, sharp and terrible as a clap of thunder, had brought something new into the world. A dark apparition slips forward wherever the poets turn—a shadow known as temptation. Nothing galls Mara like the thought that somewhere, somehow, some son or daughter will get free.

These poems, sung again and again in the teeth of temptation, were composed by women and men who struggled heroically to see through the vanities life holds out. The poets resort again and again to the simple insight of the Buddha: impermanence. "The world is impermanent, it passes away, there is no refuge." And with touching simplicity they notice how blessed they are to be born then, there, in northern India at a time when a living Buddha—to them a sharp-minded, undeniably human teacher, witty enough to outwit millennia of prejudice and ignorance—walked the earth.

ANDREW SCHELLING
Boulder, Colorado
May 1995

Glossary

ARHAT (Skt.)   A disciple of the Buddha who has achieved irreversible insight.

BHIKKHU (Pali)   A celibate wandering Buddhist alms-seeker.

BHIKKHUNI (Pali)   The feminine form of the word *bhikkhu*.

BRAHMIN (Skt.)   A member of the priestly caste in Hinduism, often depicted in Buddhist literature as stiff, ritualistic officers of the old regime.

BUDDHA-AGE   Throughout vast stretches of time and in every universe, buddhas, or "wakened ones," have appeared. Any period in which a buddha appears is termed a Buddha-age, or Buddha-era.

DHARMA (Skt.)   The truth, or law; specifically, the teachings of the Buddha.

DHYANA (Skt.)   Meditation.

JAINISM   One of the old yogic traditions of India. It stresses noninjury and the performance of meritorious asceticism.

KAMALOKA (Skt.)   The realm of desire; colloquially, this world, the one ruled by passion and lust.

KASI (Pali; Skt.: Kashi)   The present-day city of Banares.

LOKAPALA (Skt.)   A protector of place, a local guardian, an indigenous spirit power.

MANTRA (Skt.)   Mind protector, a symbolic arrangement of syllables or words with charged meaning, used for contemplation and repeatedly recited by the practitioner.

MARA (Skt.)   From the same Indo-European root that forms *mortal* or *mortuary*, Mara is the name of death personified, or death-in-life—the great tempter of the Buddhist world, who entered into a mighty wizard-battle with the Buddha on the eve of his enlightenment and was vanquished. But Mara remains the bane of the committed practitioner.

MOUNT MERU   Sacred mountain, the center of the Buddhist cosmos.

NIBBANA (Pali; Skt.: *nirvana*)   Literally "blown out," the extinction of delusions and cravings, often depicted as the blowing out of a lamp.

NIGANTHAS (Pali)   Lit. "freed from all fetters." Epithet for a follower of the Jain tradition.

PRETA (Skt.)   A hungry ghost. *Pretas* have mountainous bellies and thin necks and are possessed by insatiable craving. They inhabit the hungry ghost realm, one of the six Buddhist realms of existence.

RAHU (Skt.)   The celestial demon, or dragon, that pursues the moon, causing eclipses by repeatedly swallowing it.

SAMSARA (Skt.)   Literally "the flowing world," the world of phenomena and rebirth. Existentially, *samsara* is the condition from which one departs for *nirvana*.

SADHU (Skt.)   Lit. "one who goes straight to the goal." A wandering renunciant in the Hindu tradition, generally a worshipper of the god Shiva.

SANGHA (Skt.)   The spiritual community of Buddhist recluses. Later the Sangha came to include laypeople and even all sentient beings. It is one of the Three Jewels of Buddhism, along with the Buddha and the Dharma.

SHAKYAMUNI (Skt.)   Epithet of the Buddha: "sage of the Shakya clan."

SIDDHARTHA GAUTAMA (Skt.)   Given name of the young prince who became "Buddha" or "wakened one." Also referred to as Gautama Buddha after his enlightenment.

TATHAGATA (Skt.)   "Thus Come" or "Thus Gone"; an epithet of the Buddha, meaning He Who Has Passed Through, or maybe He Who Leaves No Trace.

THREE BRANCHES   *Shila, dhyana,* and *prajna,* the three activities the Buddhist practitioner cultivates, namely, conduct, meditation, and wisdom.

VIHARA (Skt.)   Originally, a forest grove, city park, or retreat center, the word literally means "place to wander about." Eventually *vihara* came to refer to the vast monastic colleges strung across northern India, where contemplatives, artists, and philosophers gathered.

Bibliography

Basham, A. L. *The Wonder That Was India.* Third edition. New York: Taplinger, 1968.

Murcott, Susan. *The First Buddhist Women.* Berkeley, Calif.: Parallax Press, 1991.

Norman, K. R. *Elders' Verses.* London: Pali Text Society, 1971.

Oldenberg, Hermann, and Richard Pischel, eds. *The Thera- and Theri-Gatha.* Second edition. London: Pali Text Society, 1966.

Ray, Reginald A. *Buddhist Saints in India: A Study in Buddhist Values and Orientations.* New York: Oxford University Press, 1994.

Rhys Davids, Caroline A. F. *Psalms of the Early Buddhists.* London: Pali Text Society, 1909.

———. *To Become or Not to Become (That Is the Question!).* London: Luzac & Co., 1937.

Rhys Davids, T. W., and William Stede. *The Pali Text Society's Pali-English Dictionary.* London: Pali Text Society, 1921.

Sankiccha, Rahula, et al., eds. *Thera-Gatha.* Rangoon: Uttam Bhikshu, 1937.

Schelling, Andrew. *The India Book: Essays and Translations from Indian Asia.* Oakland, Calif.: O Books, 1993.

About the Translators and the Artist

ANNE WALDMAN is an internationally known poet. In 1974, she and Allen Ginsberg founded the Jack Kerouac School of Disembodied Poetics at The Naropa Institute in Boulder, Colorado, where she continues to serve on the faculty. She is the author of numerous books of poetry and editor of several poetics anthologies, including *The Beat Book: Poems and Fiction from the Beat Generation* and (with Andrew Schelling) *Disembodied Poetics, Annals of the Jack Kerouac School.*

ANDREW SCHELLING is a poet, essayist, and translator who has traveled extensively in India and the Himalayas. His books include *Old Growth: Poems and Notebooks 1986–1994* and *Dropping the Bow: Poems of Ancient India.* He has been awarded the Academy of American Poets Translation Prize and a Witter Bynner Foundation for Poetry grant for translation. He is on the faculty of The Naropa Institute in Boulder, Colorado, where he teaches poetry, Sanskrit, and wilderness writing.

ROBERT SCHELLING is a sculptor whose work has been influenced by his travels in India where he studied casting techniques used in making traditional sacred objects. He has also studied art and anthropology at the University of California at Berkeley. Schelling teaches sculpture and drawing at Clark University in Worcester, Massachusetts.